GETTING EVEN
WITH THE
ANSWERING MACHINE

JOHN CARFI & CLIFF CARLE

Illustrated by Greg Tenorio

CCC Publications • Los Angeles

Published by

CCC PUBLICATIONS
18129 Delano Street
Reseda, CA 91335
(818) 705-5556

Manufactured in the
United States of America

Cover design & illustrations © 1985
CCC Publications

ISBN: 0-918259-01-0

First printing—September 1985

ABOUT THE AUTHORS

After flunking out of Mortician's School for eating "pizza-with-everything" during autopsies, CLIFF CARLE and JOHN CARFI became comedy writers. Both have written for BIG NAME comedians (who must remain anonymous because their lawyers said so). In addition, John Carfi is a stand-up comedian who headlines in the TOP CLUBS around the country and appears on television. Cliff Carle and John Carfi both live in L.A. Their minds are elsewhere.

—CONTENTS—

—INTRODUCTION—

In the beginning there was the boring message. Many a prehistoric man returned from a hard day battling dinosaurs only to find no one had left a return message on his cave wall.

About a million years later, NO HANG-UPS (Funny Answering Machine Messages) was written to solve the problem of dull outgoing messages. Soon, ordinary machine owners everywhere were evolving into comedians, virtually overnight. And, after putting jokes in their outgoing messages, answering machines became less intimidating and more acceptable in today's modern society.

In spite of the success of NO HANG-UPS, there are still thousands of boring and prehistoric outgoing messages in existence today. Therefore, this book was written for the **caller.** Now you can be a comic and leave funny messages when you reach a humdrum machine.

DIRECTIONS (How To Use This Book)

A) Knowing when your friends are usually out, call with a message in mind—if you **do** reach a human, save it for next time.

B) If you reach a machine unexpectedly, leave a normal message (name and number), then call right back with a gag message from the book.

ADULTS: 2–3 messages every 4 hours—or as needed. Do not exceed maximum dosage of 8 messages per day. If jaw muscles become sore, or rash develops, consult a physician.

WARNING: Keep messages out of reach of small children—if swallowed or memorized, induce vomiting.

IMPORTANT: Keep laughing!

—John Carfi
&
Cliff Carle

P.S. For easier readability, we have used the generic names "JANE" and "JOHN." Just substitute either your name or the machine owner's name where appropriate. Also, we have used a generic telephone number (123-4567). Substitute your own number if the person you are calling has a sense of humor.

[NOTE: "Getting Even With The Answering Machine" was written in the "spirit of fun." If you reach one of the more serious machine owners, we suggest you add the tag "just kidding" or call back and let them know you were only joking.]

1

FAMOUS MESSAGES

This is Dirty Harry. Wanna make my day?
Change your message, punk!

CLICK

Hi. This is Richard Simmoms. Please give me a call at:
1 and 2 and 3—and 4 and 1 and 2 and 3. Come on! Let's get that ugly cellulite off those index fingers!
That's 1 and 2 and 3—and. . .ETC.

CLICK

Hi. This is Marie Antoinette. What a funny message! I laughed my head off!

CLICK

Hello. This is Santa Claus. I'm calling to tell you that I won't be stopping by this year. I joined ZZ Top and I'm going on tour.

CLICK

Hi. This is The Invisible Man. Can you recommend a doctor? I have a serious problem. Everything I eat goes right through me!

CLICK

Hi. This is Jean Trixon with your daily horoscope:
"You are gullible, naive, and people often take advantage of you." That concludes your fortune. Please send me five hundred bucks!

CLICK

Hi. This is Julia Children. I've got a dish that will melt in your mouth—an uncooked TV Dinner!

CLICK

5

Hello. This is the Surgeon General. I have determined that your message is hazardous to my health.

CLICK

Hi. This is Dr. Christian Barnyard. What an inspiring message! I'll keep it next to my hearts!

CLICK

(HAPPY VOICE)
This is Dr. Jeckle—I love your message!
(ANGRY VOICE)
This is Mr. Hyde—I hate your message!

CLICK

(OPTION: MAKE TWO CALLS)

6

(WHILE EATING AN APPLE)
Hi. This is Liz. I had a great message I was going to leave you, but I got hungry and ate it.

CLICK

Hi. This is the Amazing Kresgin. I'm sorry. I must have dialed the wrong number.

CLICK

My fellow answering machine owner, this is Tricky Dicky. I was wondering—do you have an extra tape? Mine is *still* missing!

CLICK

Hello. This is Harry Lorayne, famous memory expert. You just won a free six-week memory course. To confirm, please call me at 123-45. . .
Uh? let's see. . .
is it 67? or 76???

CLICK

Hey, man! This is Sammy Davids Jr. Looks like I missed you again, but I'll keep an eye out for ya!

CLICK

This is Evil K. Nevill. I'm calling the agent for Fall-State. This is the tenth time! I don't know why you're not returning my calls. I told you all I want is car insurance!

CLICK

Hello. This is Icabod Crane. I'm calling to promote my new book: "How To Get Ahead."

CLICK

Hi. This is Mary Lou Retfig. I really *flipped* over your message!

CLICK

CHRISTMAS CALL:

Hi. This is Santa Claus.
You better not pout,
You better not cry,
You better watch out,
I'm telling you why:
Your message sucks reindeer doo-doo!

CLICK

RATED "PG"

Hi! I'm so excited! This is my first time ever leaving a message on a machine! I hope I'm good and live up to your expectations! Well, here we go:
My number is 123. . .
(EMBARRASSED)
Whoops, sorry! Pre-mature message!

CLICK

Hello? This is the apartment manager. Due to numerous complaints from your neighbors, I'm going to have to ask you to put shock absorbers on your bed!

CLICK

You know, some cops are so mean! Earlier, I was in a phone booth talking dirty to my girl. This officer comes over and pounds on the door—so we had to put on our clothes and leave!

CLICK

Hey JOHN, I hear your sex life's been lousy lately—guess you'll just have to take matters into your own hands!

CLICK

Hi. I need your advice. I'm a 65-year-old flasher. I've been exposing myself now on the street and in parks for the past 30 years. What do you think—should I retire? Or stick it out another year?

CLICK

Hello. This is the Pharmacy calling. I wanted to confirm an order we received over the phone earlier today for a case of "Reparation H." Now, it says here, you want it delivered to your back door???

CLICK

Hello. This is the Sperm Bank. Due to infrequent deposits, we're going to have to close your account.

CLICK

Hello? JOHN's answering machine? This is JANE's answering machine. I hear you're a real electronic stud and generate a lot of voltage. Tell ya what—I'll show you my tape if you show me yours!

CLICK

(SEXY VOICE)
Hi. This may sound like a real sensual, *orgasmic* message—but I'm only faking it.

CLICK

Hey JOHN—got a hot tip on a new girl in town—just your type—she's really loose. No kidding, she hangs out in single's bars with a birth control pill taped to her lip!

CLICK

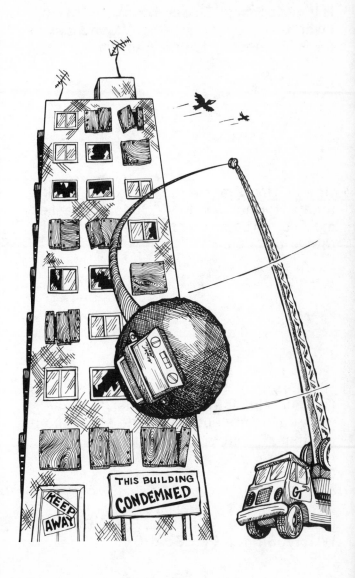

THIS BUILDING
CONDEMNED

KEEP
AWAY

GT

Is this Mr. Smith? This is your dentist calling.
I wanted to remind you that Wednesday at
5:00 I'm suppose to drill your wife.

CLICK

Hey JOHN, I met this really sexy bookie
today. Her name is Mary Odds. She asked
me if I'd run some numbers for her. I said I'd
rather lay odds.

CLICK

Hi. I got your number off a restroom wall and
I'm definitely interested in the "kinky sex"
you promised—but I'm a little leary about
the thing with the live moose.

CLICK

(OPTION: HAVE A COUPLE FRIENDS CALL
WITH A SIMILAR MESSAGE)

Hi, JANE. This is JOHN. The good news is, last night you were fantastic. The bad news is, I'm calling from the clinic.

CLICK

Hey JOHN, I was just talking to this lady, Suzie Sleazolla. I asked if she liked **fore**-play—she said, "The more guys the merrier!" If you're interested, give me a call.

CLICK

Hello. This is JANE, the girl you met at that wild surprise party eight months ago. Well, in about a month, I'll have another surprise for you. . .

CLICK

(MECHANICAL VOICE)
Hello? JOHN's answering machine? This is JANE's answering machine. I get so excited when I reach you—my transistors turn red, my capacitors enlarge and my diodes get hot! I can't wait until someone gets home and touches my knobs. What a turn on!

CLICK

NIGHT MESSAGE:

Hello, JOHN? This is JANE. It's late and I'm lying here on my bed in my sheerest, most revealing negligee. The lights are dimmed and I've poured the champagne. I was wondering if you would like to come over and climb on top of my...*roof*—and adjust the antenna. I can't get Johnny to come in clear.

CLICK

(COUPLE DEEP BREATHS)
Hhhhhh... Hhhhh...
Hi. I'm returning your heavy breathing...And by the way, may I suggest a breath mint!

CLICK

I met this girl at a singles' bar last night. I think she might be a little loose—she knows the entire CITY football team and their *playing positions*—and I don't mean on the field!

CLICK

Hi. This is JOHN. Since I last talked to you I started dating this Olympic swimmer. Last night I wanted to go to bed—she wanted to go swimming. So we compromised—we got in the pool and spawned.

CLICK

PHONEy SOLICITORS

Hello and congratulations! You've been selected to be a member of the City Beautification Committee. Your job is to keep out of sight!

CLICK

Hello. This is Jose's Gardening Service. We grow the best roses because we use the freshest manure. I am leaving a sample in your mailbox.

CLICK

Hi. This is the new Punk Beauty Salon. You've won a free facial, including massage—but give us a couple days, our air hammer broke down.

CLICK

Hi. This is the Burnum and Barley Circus. When you were young, did you fantasize about joining the circus when you grew up? Well, now's your chance—our geek quit! Call 123-4567 for information.

CLICK

Hello. This is the Telephone Dating Service. We've computed your perfect match. For your date we suggest you dress casual, be on time, and if you plan to go to the park or beach, bring a leash.

CLICK

This is the City Zoo. We know where you're hiding out. Are you going to come quietly— or do we bring a net?

CLICK

Hello. This is the Department of Offense. You have been selected at random by computer to participate in a nuclear test which will be held in Nevada this weekend. Just to be safe, please bring your sunglasses and some bandaids.

CLICK

Hello. This is the Organ Transplant Bank—
your brain is ready.

CLICK

Hello. I'm with the Casualty Company and
we're offering a new policy called "Answering Machine Insurance." It covers your
machine during times like this when your
message is a total loss.

CLICK

(TWO PEOPLE TALKING
SIMULTANEOUSLY)
Hi. We're the Siamese Twins Tailors. We
make clothes for couples who are really
close, if you know what we mean. Our specialty is quadruple-knit sweaters. And you
Siamese ballerinas will love our snug-fitting
four-fours! Call 123-4567.

CLICK

Hi. This is all-new Bob's Airline. You're the winner of our "Grand Opening" Sweepstakes! Your prize is a free trip to Hawaii! Oh, one problem, we don't have our planes yet, so we will have to drive you.

CLICK

Hello. This is the National Charities Advertising Division. Congratulations! You've been named the poster-boy for Hemorrhoids!

CLICK

Hello. This is the Outer Space Travel Agency. We are taking applications for civilian passengers on the Space Shuttle and someone sent in your name and a current photo. On seeing your picture, we've decided to reject the application—we don't want to give alien life the wrong impression!

CLICK

Hello. This is the Sure-Kill Poison Company. We'd like to use your picture on our bottles.

CLICK

Hello. This is the Oriental Laundry. We lost your clothes—but we have many photos of them.

CLICK

Hello. This is the Pessimistic Travel Agency. Feeling bad because you have no time for a vacation? Well, for a small fee, we'll send you photos of your favorite vacation spot experiencing bad weather. See tornadoes, hailstorms, major wind damage and floods. Plus, your favorite hotel in the background with a "no vacancy" sign. That's the Pessimistic Travel Agency—"A Great Way To Stay Away!"

CLICK

NIGHT CALL

This is the Cemetery calling. We just wanted to remind you that you have to be back before sunrise.

CLICK

(SERIOUS)
Hello. I'm calling from the "Save The Snails" Foundation. Every year thousands of defenseless snails are marinated with French cheeses, cooked in sweet butter sauce, then put on crystal plates and sprinkled lightly with garlic and seasoned pepper...
uh, listen, I'm gonna have to call you back after my lunch break...

CLICK

Hi. This is Walt Dizzy Productions calling. Are you busy today? Trinkerbell called in sick and we need a fairy.

CLICK

Hi. This is the City Pound. We're trying to find a home for a cute little puppy—it's a Mexican Chihauhau—his name is "Future Burrito." He's very easy to train. Whenever he misbehaves, just hold up a tortilla. Call 123-4567.

CLICK

Hello. This is the Darwin Foundation. We're currently running tests to prove conclusively that man evolved from apes. Several people volunteered your name as a research subject.
Please call 123-4567.

CLICK

Hello. This is the Ring-A-Ling Brothers' Circus. One of our clowns quit and we're offering you the job—not because you're funny—we've seen the way you dress!

CLICK

Hi. This is your local used car salesman. Have I got a beauty for you: a 1955 Desoto— mint condition! The previous owner, who recently died and was cremated, absolutely loved this car! One catch—his remains are in the ashtray. . .

CLICK

Hi. I'm starting a foundation to help people who've lost their way in life and can't seem to find themselves. I'm calling it the Jimmy Haffa House.

CLICK

Hello. This is the Beruit Travel Agency. You just won a free vacation to sunny Lebanon! You'll be staying at the lovely Crossfire Hotel bordering Israel. There's all kinds of recreation planned from "bullet ducking" to "tank dodging"! Bring plenty of Bactime and extra plasma! By the way, your stay could be indefinite.

CLICK

Hello. This is the Telephone Dating Service. We feel a man should have a girl to give him love, companionship, and emotional support—and preferably, *each girl* from a different town. Call 123-4567 for info.

CLICK

Hi. This is the Alternative Dental Association. We're calling to introduce you to all-new "Punk Dentistry":
• No anaesthesia is used.
• We promote and encourage screaming.
• The drill bit is dull, and the dentist is blind!
For further information, call 123-4567.

CLICK

Hello. This is the Post Office. If you're interested, we have a job opening. One of our
employees came out of his coma, so we had
to let him go.

CLICK

Hello. This is Cannibal's Restaurant. Today's
specials are:
- Elbows Au' Gratin
- Hand-On-Rye
- All-Caucasian Patty
- Barbie-cued
- Ladies' Fingers
- Footlongs (sizes 11½ and up!)
- And our ever-popular "Leg-Of-Larry."
- For dessert: "Eyes-cream"!
That's Cannibal's—the restaurant that brings
new meaning to "Hot Cross Buns"! Call 123-
4567 for reservations.

CLICK

"BLUE SKY" PRODUCTS

Hello. I'm a telephone salesperson with "Blue Sky Products"—the company that specializes in products you can't live without! Today's special is our deluxe "lip warmers." They come in three sizes: *small, medium,* and *Mick Jogger*—for problem lips. Call 123-4567. Order today and get big discounts on our "foot gloss," "nose-hair curlers" and the "front scratcher."

CLICK

Hello. This is Blue Sky again—B.S. for short, with more products you can't live without. Today's B.S. specials are:

- "Shake & Bake" for sushi.
- For extremely fat people, a bathroom scale made out of Hershey's chocolate.
- For people who are cheaper than cheap, we have "imitation rhinestones."
- And "mono headphones"—for people with a one-track mind.

Call 123-4567.

CLICK

Hello. This is Blue Sky Products. Tired of feeling stupid? Tired of white skin? Well, now you can get smart and get a tan at the same time with "IQ-T." Just put a little on your forehead and instantly you'll get a brilliant tan! That's IQ-T! Call 123-4567.

CLICK

Hello. This is Blue Sky Products—B.S. for short. Are you so overweight that to get into your health spa you have to have a two-for-one pass? When you breakdance, does everything get broken? Well, why waste time dieting when you can instantly *look* like you lost weight with all-new "Circus Mirror Sequins." Just sprinkle thousands of these tiny circus mirrors over your clothing and give the illusion of being incredibly thin. Now you can pig out as much as you want with "Circus Mirror Sequins"! Call 123-4567.

CLICK

Hello. Blue Sky Products again. Are you overweight and *proud* of it? Then you'll probably be interested in these new B.S. non-health products:
● Food-flavor lip gloss.
● Blueberry pancake make-up.
● And, our really *big* seller, "Oil Of O'Large."
Call 123-4567.

CLICK

Hello. This is Blue Sky Products, again. Is sex with your spouse like a ride on a roller coaster? It lasts two minutes and you get sick afterwards! Well, try new "TY-ONE-ON," the pain tablets that instantly *give you a headache!* That's TY-ONE-ON, for the perfect excuse not to have sex! Call 123-4567.

CLICK

Hello. This is Blue Sky again. Our latest product is a transistor radio with 500 pound headphones. It's called a Soney "I-Can't-Walkman."

CLICK

TRICKS "R" US

(RADIO ANNOUNCER VOICE)
Hello! This is "Dialing For Bucks"! $1000 is yours and all you have to do is call us back at 123-45(MUMBLE). That's 123-45(MUMBLE)!

CLICK

Hi. This is JANE. You might be able to reach me at 157-2137. If not, try 061-0728. If that number is busy, try 102-1863 or 026-5180. Now, if you get a service instead of me, hang up and dial 172-8750 or 061-0936. Better yet, try 191-3983. If I'm not there, I'll be at the telephone company, getting my number changed.

CLICK

Hello. This is the No-Tell Motel. Congratulations, Mr. John Smith! You've won our "Customer-Of-The-Year" Award!

CLICK

Hi. I'd like to show you a little trick: Okay, I'm going to leave this message blindfolded and with both hands tied behind my back. Ready: "Help! I've been robbed!"

CLICK

Here, JANE. Machine your, funny sounds. Better it, take fixed, to be. Talk to, later you.

CLICK

This is the Specialty Shipping Company. Our truck broke down this morning in front of your house and our cargo, about 30,000 laboratory fleas, escaped onto your property. After careful consideration, we've decided you may keep them.

CLICK

Hi. I'm calling from a phone booth and I. . .uh, wait a minute—there's a guy outside with a big red "S" on his chest—wants in here real bad! I'll call ya back later!

CLICK

HELLO-hello, JOHN-john. THERE-there SEEMS-seems TO-to BE-be A-a STRANGE-strange ECHO-echo IN-in YOUR-your MACHINE-machine.

CLICK

Hi. I was going to ask you for a date, but during your message I heard a "scratching" noise in the background and I thought, "Hmmm. . .nice girl, but *that* itch!"

CLICK

(FAST)
Hi. I'm rushing out the door, but I wanted to let you know that a bunch of us are going out to a great new place tonight! There'll be good food, great band, dancing and plenty of single women. So, if you're interested, we'll meet you there.

CLICK

(PROFESSIONAL RADIO VOICE)
...4567! Dial that number now and find out about the brand-new Mercedes you won!

CLICK

Hello. This is the IRS. We know how much you make. We were wondering what it must be like to have all that money—and come April 15th, we're gonna find out.

CLICK

Hey JOHN, about that money I owe you—I just called to tell ya I'll be paying it back in *three* days...January 5th, July 6th, and December 7th.

CLICK

(OPTION: CALL A BUSINESS CREDITOR WHO HAS AN ANSWERING MACHINE ON WHEN THEY ARE OUT.)

OFFICE GAG:

DAY I:

HAVE 3 OR 4 CO-WORKERS CALL YOUR
FRIEND'S MACHINE AND AD LIB:
• Hello? Hello? Hello?
• Hey JOHN, I can barely hear your mes-
  sage!
• JOHN? Turn up your machine, man!
• What? Talk louder, man—can't hear you!
ETC.

DAY II:

(BY THE NEXT DAY, OF COURSE, THE
MACHINE OWNER WILL HAVE MADE AN
ADJUSTMENT ON HIS MACHINE.) HAVE 3
OR 4 CO-WORKERS CALL AND AD LIB:
• Hey JOHN, your message is too loud!
• Turn it down, man, you almost broke my
  eardrums!
• What are you shouting for, JOHN!
ETC.

CALL #1:

Hello. This is the laundry—we lost your shirt!

CLICK

CALL #2:

Hello. This is your broker—you lost your shirt!

CLICK

CALL #3:

Help! This is your shirt—I'm lost.

CLICK

IDENTIFY YOURSELF AND START TELLING
YOUR FAVORITE JOKE—BUT CUT YOUR-
SELF OFF (CLICK DISCONNECT BUTTON
A COUPLE TIMES) AND HANG UP JUST
BEFORE THE PUNCHLINE.

Hey JOHN, how'd ya like to go to a free Rock
Festival? Meet us tomorrow at 6:00 outside
the Geological Institute!

CLICK

(PAUSE BRIEFLY ON EACH DASH)
Hi. This is --ANE. I'm not --ure, but I think
there's --omething wrong with your --achine.
Anyway, give me a --all at one two --hree,
four --ive six --even. (OR YOUR NUMBER
LEAVING OUT FIRST CONSONANTS).
Thank --ou.

CLICK

Hi. You probably don't realize it, but I'm performing an incredible magic trick right now, on your machine. I'm actually leaving **two** messages at once. . .my first—and my last!

CLICK

(PLACE HANDKERCHIEF OVER RECEIVER)
Hi. Can you guess who this is?
Nope! Guess again. . .
Nope! Guess again. . .
Aw, that was close! Guess again. . .
Nope! Guess again. . .
(CONTINUE FOR AS LONG AS YOU WANT—
EVEN CALL BACK AND CONTINUE IF THE
MACHINE HAS A LIMITED TAPE AND CUTS
YOU OFF.)

CLICK

Hey JOHN. Want to hear the world's funniest Pollock joke? Just dial 976-POLZ.

CLICK

49

"THINKETTES"

Just wondering. . .
if you eat a TV Dinner then throw up, is it called "bad reception"?

CLICK

Just wondering. . .
back in the days of the Roman Empire, do
you think a kid ever said to his father, "Dad,
can I borrow the chariot?"

CLICK

Just wondering. . .
if a teenage bull misbehaved and his parents
sent him to his pen—would he be "grounded
beef"?

CLICK

Just wondering. . .
if Joan got fat, would Liz become a comedian?

CLICK

Just wondering. . .
what if a word in the dictionary was
mispelled—how would we know?

CLICK

Just wondering. . .
who do you suppose goes out and puts all
those *old shoes* along the side of the free-
way?

CLICK

Just wondering. . .
if God took acid, would he see people?

CLICK

I saw a group of Oriental tourists today. Every one of them had cameras. I was wondering. . .
if the Theory of Evolution holds true, a hundred years from now, do you think Oriental children will be born with a built-in flash?

CLICK

Remember. . .
never say to a transplant patient, "Did you have a change of heart?"—just kidneying!

CLICK

SPECIAL DELIVERIES
(For Typical Messages)

AFTER "LEAVE A MESSAGE AT THE SOUND OF THE TONE":

(POMPOUS VOICE)
"Leave a message at the sound of the tone? The *tone*? You call that puny noise a tone? It might pass for a "beep" or a "buzz" but I certainly wouldn't classify it as a *tone*! You get a regulation tone—I'll leave a message.

CLICK

AFTER "LEAVE YOUR NAME, NUMBER, AND A MESSAGE":

Hi. I don't know who I am—I forget my number and my message is a secret, so I can't tell.

CLICK

AFTER "LEAVE YOUR NAME AND NUMBER":

My name? *JANE.*
My number? I'm a *"10."*

CLICK

AFTER "LEAVE YOUR NAME, NUMBER, AND A MESSAGE":

My name? My number? A message? Sorry, I'm not into Trivia.

CLICK

56

TO PERSON WHO LEAVES SAME
MESSAGE ON MACHINE:

They say crime doesn't pay? Well, I'll give
you ten bucks to change that message—it's
killing me!

CLICK

TO PERSON WHO LEAVES SAME
MESSAGE ON MACHINE:

Hey JOHN, I don't know what's going on, but
everytime your message plays, dust and a
musty odor comes out of my receiver...

CLICK

TO PERSON WHO LEAVES SAME
MESSAGE ON MACHINE:

Guiness calling. Okay! Okay! You've got the
world's record for longest running answering
machine message—so change it already!

CLICK

AFTER CORNY OR BLAND MESSAGE:

Hi. Have you ever heard that old saying, "If you don't have something nice to say, don't say anything?"
(PAUSE)

CLICK

AFTER CORNY OR BLAND MESSAGE:

I was so depressed today . . .
at first I was gonna jump off an 80 story building and land on a bed of poison-tipped spears. Or, maybe drink nitro-glycerin and do a dying-swan into a vat of scalding hot oil while holding a 10,000 volt electric wire in my teeth. Nah—not horrible enough! Then I thought, "I know, I'll call JOHN's machine and listen to his message!"

CLICK

AFTER CORNY MESSAGE:

That message was so funny I forgot to laugh. I also forgot to leave my name and number.

CLICK

AFTER CORNY MESSAGE:

Ugh! You oughta give noseplugs with that message!

CLICK

AFTER LONG OUTGOING MESSAGE:

What a message! I clapped all through it! I had to do something to stay awake.

CLICK

AFTER LONG OUTGOING MESSAGE:

(SNORING SOUND)
Zzzzz ... Zzzzz ...

CLICK

TO PERSON WHO SCREENS THEIR
INCOMING MESSAGES:

(RECORD ON TAPE WITH FRIEND SOME
SENSUAL MOANS AND GROANS)
Mmmmmm . . . Ahhhh . . . Ohhhhh . . . . ETC.
Hi. I called to invite you to join our wild orgy
over here, but I guess you're not home . . .
(HANG UP EVEN IF THEY PICK UP)

CLICK

TO PERSON WHO CHANGES THEIR
MESSAGE TOO FREQUENTLY:

I notice your message is different every day—
it's good to see you don't make the same
mistake twice!

CLICK

AFTER MESSAGE LEFT BY
ASPIRING ACTOR:

Uh, don't call us—we'll call you.

CLICK

MESSAGE FOR A BALD FRIEND:

(READ LIKE A TELEGRAM)
Hi. I'm at the Barber Shop.
Having a great time.
Wish you had hair.
Yours, JOHN.

CLICK

TO MARRIED COUPLE:

You know, I just figured out that if you have a
new baby it will probably look just like you.
But don't worry, it won't stay wrinkled and
bald for long.

CLICK

AFTER CALLING EACH OTHER'S
MACHINES WITHOUT CONNECTING:

Hi JANE. I'm returning the call you left on my
machine from when I called your machine
because of the previous message you left
on my machine about the original message I
left on your machine—except now I forget
why I called in the first place? ? ?

CLICK

SELF ABUSEMENT

(DRUNKEN VOICE)
Hi. This is JANE. If you have any idea as to
my whereabouts, please give me a call.

CLICK

(TALK VERY SLOW)
Hello?... JOHN?... It's... JANE...
You... know... I... guess... I...
should've... called... first... *then*...
took... the... tranquilizers...

CLICK

Hi. I just got back from Vegas and boy am I
frustrated! I go up to this machine, put in
quarters, pull the handle back—put in quarters, pull the handle back, put in *more* quarters, pull the handle back! Finally, after 50
dollars, I get my cigarettes!

CLICK

Hello? Is this Bob's Appliance Center? Listen,
my ex-wife, who I'm still on speaking terms
with, said I might get a better tan if I stick my
head in the microwave. I was wonderin' if
you might know what setting to put it on.

CLICK

Hi JANE. I called to tell you I finally met my "Superman." We spent the night together—but it turned out he was faster than a speeding bullet!

CLICK

Hello. This is JANE. I called to see if you could recommend a good answering machine. I think my old one was made by "Mission Implausible"—when I turned it on it burst into flames.

CLICK

Hello? Is this Dear Blabby? I need some advice! I don't know what to do ? ? ? I found out this girl I'm dating is seeing another man. Then it turns out she's been with him for five years. What makes it even worse, he's her husband!

CLICK

Hi JOHN. I was just sitting here smoking a joint and I suddenly came up with the world's funniest joke:
Two guys walk into a bar—no wait, three guys—no! eighty penguins!—wait—it wasn't a bar, it was a sperm bank—and they weren't walking, they were snorting cream cheese—no, wait—uh, I'll get back to ya!

CLICK

Hi JANE. You know that guy I've been trying to get to ask me out for over a year? Well, he finally treated me to a drive-in movie—unfortunately, he made me take my own car!

CLICK

Hi. This is JOHN. Last night I met this real foxy lady at a single's bar. She was an artist. Unfortunately, when I hit on her, she gave me the brush-off.

CLICK

Hi. I have to go to Detroit. You know, I read some statistics that said the odds of getting shot and killed there are 1 in 5—whereas the odds of getting shot twice there are 1 in 10,000. So, as soon as I get there, I'm gonna shoot myself in the leg.

CLICK

(BROKEN ENGLISH)
Hi. I am in your country only few days and do not understand your customs. Can you tell me please why last night I have problem at disco? I only follow instruction! I am dancing goodly and someone yell "get down!"—so I lay on floor—people step on me—I scream— they throw me out of disco!

CLICK

Hello, JANE. We have to talk! Everytime my husband comes back from a business trip, there's another notch carved into the handle of his briefcase!

CLICK

67

(GROGGY)
Hey JOHN, what a party last night! I never drank so much in my entire life! By the way, I'm curious—did I have a good time?

CLICK

(INSECURE)
I know a real funny joke, but I'm not going to tell you—you'd only laugh at me!

CLICK

(NORMAL VOICE)
Hello. I am a lawyer with the FCC. I'm calling to inform you that the "beep" tone on your answering machine is in violation of code. Your particular frequency has been found to cause almost immediate sterilization in some men . . .
(HIGH VOICE)
If you do not take your machine in and have the "beep" frequency changed, we will be forced to prosecute. Thank you.

CLICK

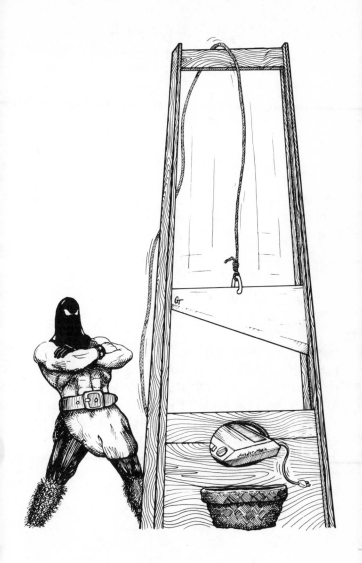

CRACKPOTS & CRAZIES

Hello. I'm a new plastic surgeon in town. I've opened a new clinic, but even with major discounts, I can't seem to get any business, and I haven't a clue why ? ? ? So, if you or a friend have considered plastic surgery, I'm offering a *free* consultation visit. Just call 123-4567 and ask for Dr. Potatohead.

CLICK

Hello, kind sir or madam. This is the new Obsequious Weather Bureau calling. We feel so bad! There's been a change in the weather. Last night we predicted clear skies, but now it looks like rain—so we're calling **everyone** in the phone-book to apologize. We're really sorry!

CLICK

(NERVOUS)
Hello. Uh, I'm a new undertaker, just out of school, and I'm starting up a new cemetery. Anyway, I, uh, heard you're not feeling well and I really wanted to get this thing off the ground—uh, I hope I'm not being too pushy, but, uh, why don't ya drop in sometime, okay?

CLICK

(WEARY)
Hi. This is a total stranger. I am recovering from a forefinger injury and as part of my doctor-prescribed physical therapy, every-day I have to dial all the numbers in the phonebook.
Talk to ya tomorrow!

CLICK

Hi. I can't tell you who I am, but this weekend I'm holding a meeting at my house for people like myself who suffer from paranoia. But since I don't know you that well, I better not tell you where I live.

CLICK

Hello, and please stick 'em up! I am an ago-raphobic burglar, so I have to rob people by phone. Please put all your valuables into a great big envelope and mail them to me—and please, no C.O.D's!

CLICK

Hi. This is Dr. Ben, from the new Looney-Ben Asylum. This week we're having our "Grand Opening" Special:
- Buy one lobotomy—get one free!
- Half off on straight jackets!
- Plus, all the tranquilizers you can eat!

Bring the whole family! You've got to be insane to pass up these crazy bargains!

CLICK

Hello. As you know, all public places have two restrooms—one for men and one for women. We are the Confederation of Hermaphrodites, Transexuals, Transvestites, and Ambisexuals, and we're petitioning for a *third* restroom for us. The only problem is, we can't think of a name to go on the door.

CLICK

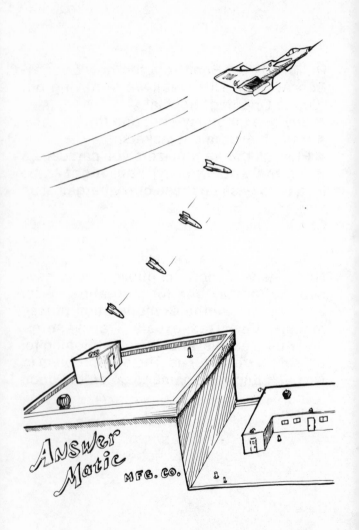

Hi. I am an amnesia victim and I just called
to say . . .
Hi. I am an amnesia victim and I just called
to say . . .
Hi. I am an amnesia victim and I just called
to say . . .
(ETC.)

CLICK

(MECHANICAL VOICE)
Hello. I am an escaped villain from the planet
Xerog. You have until moonrise to hand over
two billion Greebs or I will blow up planet
Earth!

CLICK

Hi. You don't know me. The reason I called is
because I'm trying to break my nose-picking
habit. My doctor said, when I get the urge,
stick my finger in the nearest hole seven
times.

CLICK

Hi. This is a burglar. While you were out I broke into your apartment—stole everything of value and replaced it with a cheap replica—but you'll never be able to prove it.

CLICK

Hello. This is the Department of Motor Vehicle Glove Compartments. Our department is calling your apartment to inquire about your glove compartment. Once a year your glove compartment has to be brought in to our department for inspection. You must comply immediately or our department will come to your apartment and impound your glove compartment. If you have any questions, don't call the Department of Motor Vehicle Glove Compartments—contact the Department of Apartment Owner's Glove Compartment Arguments. Thank you for your cooperation.

CLICK

THE MAD JOKESTER

(Some Old Jokes For The Corny Comic In You)

[NOTE: REALLY HAM IT UP!]

Hey! It's the **Mad Jokester!**
Why wouldn't the lady let the doctor operate on her husband?
She didn't want anyone to open her male!
Hey, what a **cut-up!**

CLICK

Hey! It's the *Mad Jokester* again!
What would you get if you crossed the Atlantic with the Titanic?
You'd get half-way!
Hey, that joke's all *wet!*

CLICK!

Hey! *Mad Jokester* here!
Why was the wagon train stuck in the middle of the prairie?
It had Injun trouble!
Hey, I should be *scalped* for that one!

CLICK

Hey! *Mad Jokester* once again!
What do you get when you cross a light-house and a hen house?
Beacon and eggs!
Hey, I'm *cookin'* now!

CLICK

Hey, it's the **Mad Jokester** checking in!
What do you get when you cross a praying
mantis and a termite?
A bug that says "grace" before eating your
house!
Hey, that one **bit the dust!**

CLICK

Hey! Heeeeeeeeeeer's the **Mad Jokester!**
What do you get when you lean a corpse up
against a doorbell?
A dead ringer!
Hey, that was **cold!** After that one, I think I
need a **stiff** drink!

CLICK

Hey! It's your old pal, the **Mad Jokester!**
Did you hear that Whurlitzer is merging
with Zerox?
Yeah, they're gonna make reproductive
organs!
Hey, that's **playing dirty!**

CLICK

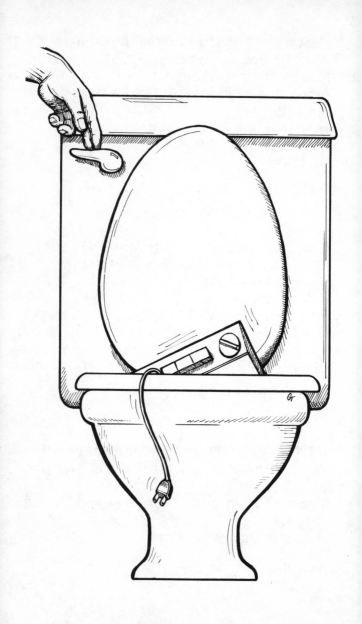

A BUNCH OF MESSAGES AT THE END OF THE BOOK

Hi. I'm taking a telephone survey. How do you feel about the Arms Race? I don't know about you, but after about 75 yards, *my* arms just peter out!

CLICK

This is the City Library. We're calling about an overdue *Geography* book you've had since 4th Grade. By now you must be an expert on the *subject,* so we don't have to tell you what *creek* you are up!

CLICK

Hello. This is your local Police Department. We're calling to warn shoppers about the armless pickpocket—this guy puts his mouth where your money is!

CLICK

Hey JOHN, can ya help me out? A friend of mine is recuperating from a transplant operation—he got one of those new artificial hearts. Anyway, I was wondering, do you think it's appropriate to send him artificial flowers?

CLICK

(DOG BARKING)
Ruff-ruff! Ruff-ruff! Ruff-ruff!
(IN BACKGROUND—MOUTH AWAY FROM RECEIVER)
Fido! How many times have I told you—that's my business phone! Use the phone in your doghouse!

CLICK

Hi. I called because . . .
uh, I forgot! Anyway, call me back later—if I remember.

CLICK

MESSAGE FOR FEBRUARY 19:

Hi. Did you know that over 100 years ago today Thomas Edison invented the phonograph? And do you know what he said the day after? "Damn! I spent seven bucks for an album and there's only *one* good song on it!"

CLICK

83

Hello? Is this the junkyard? I'm calling because a friend of mine, the "6 Million Dollar Man" walked through a lawn sprinkler, short-circuited, and now he's not worth ten cents.

CLICK

(IMITATE A CELEBRITY)
Hi JOHN. This is (CELEBRITY). Sorry you're not at home. I was going to invite you over to my wild party. All the big names are here. I'd leave my number, but, of course, it's unlisted.

CLICK

Hi. I'm calling because I'm going fishin' for compliments and I thought you might want to join me. For bait I use a dark tan and a new haircut. Yesterday I got three, but I had to throw them back—they were all too small.

CLICK

Hey, I worked out the ultimate scheme to get a great buy on furniture! You go into a furniture store, put a chair or something on Lay-Away. Go back 50 years later and pay the balance. Now you have an antique—worth five times the original price!

CLICK

I think you should either put more fire into your messages or more of your messages into the fire!

CLICK

This guy I know went in for a stomach operation. While they had him open, they were able to reach up and fix a weak heart valve at the same time. Well, I guess it's true what they say . . .
"the way to a man's heart is through his stomach!"

CLICK

Hi. I'm giving a telephone course in mind reading. Here's your first lesson: right now I'm thinking of my name and number . . .
(FIVE SECONDS OF SILENCE)
If you guessed **JANE** and **123-4567**, you're right! You passed! And now you owe me $29.95!

CLICK

Hi. I was calling to tell you about this book, "How To Torture Your Friends," but from your message, I can see you already have it.

CLICK

(RUSSIAN ACCENT)
Hello Comrade. This is "Dialing For Ruples." How much in jackpot today? You answer correct—win trip to Tahiti. You answer wrong—win trip to Siberia.

CLICK

Hello. This is Warden Smith. I'd like to thank you for volunteering for our new "Adopt-A-Hardened-Criminal" program. Your convict for a weekend is "Chainsaw Charlie," a mass murderer. When he arrives at your home, here are some helpful hints:

- No **knives** at the dinner table.
- When leaving a room he is in, always **back** out the door.
- **Hide** all your power tools.
- When showering, use the "buddy system."
- So as not to upset him, it's best not to wear **striped** pajamas.
- And finally, as for outdoor activities: Fishing . . . yes! Hunting . . . **no!**

CLICK

Hi. I'm trying to give away a cat. He'll be no problem, he's an indoor/outdoor cat—he's also machine washable!

CLICK

Hi. I'm calling to make sure you received in the mail your free sample of the new chocolate candy made in San Francisco by transvestites—it's called a "He-She" Bar.

CLICK

I notice you're having trouble with your *vowels*—have you tried a laxative?

CLICK

Hi. Thought you might want to join us for a surprise party tonight. A friend of ours just had a sex-change operation. He—or I guess it's *she,* now—tried twice unsuccessfully. But the third operation was a success. So, when he—or *she* walks in the door tonight, we're gonna hit the lights and sing, "She's once, twice, three times a lady . . . "

CLICK

AND...

Well, you've reached the end of the book. The authors, John and Cliff are out somewhere spending their money unwisely. However, if you can think of any funny responses they forgot, write them on the "Richer" & Famous Coupon (next page) along with your name and address (next, next page) and send them in. If John and Cliff think your "response" is funny enough, they will put it, along with your name, in their next book. Plus they will send you a check for $5.00—providing they don't blow all their money on party hats and wax lips.

(Submissions cannot be returned unless a self-addressed, stamped envelope is included.)

"RICHER" AND FAMOUS COUPON

YOUR MESSAGE HERE: _____

_____

_____

_____

_____

_____

_____

_____

MAIL TO:
CCC PUBLICATIONS
18129 DELANO ST.
RESEDA, CA 91335

(OVER)

GETTING EVEN WITH THE
ANSWERING MACHINE

NAME :

_____

ADDRESS:

_____

_____